CRISISPOINTS FOR WOMEN

YOU'RE BETTER THAN YOU THINK!

M A D A L E N E   H A R R I S

NAVPRESS

A MINISTRY OF THE NAVIGATORS
P.O. BOX 6000, COLORADO SPRINGS, COLORADO 80934

© 1990 by The Navigators
All rights reserved, including translation
ISBN 08910-93273

Cover illustration by Sidney Fisher.

CRISISPOINTS FOR WOMEN series edited by
Judith Couchman.

This series offers God's hope and healing for life's challenges.

All Scripture quotations in this publication are from the *Holy Bible: New International Version* (NIV). Copyright © 1973, 1978, 1984, International Bible Society. Used by permission of Zondervan Bible Publishers.

Printed in the United States of America

C O N T E N T S

To Charette
who walked with me through it all.

ACKNOWLEDGMENTS

To these people I am deeply indebted: Judith Couchman, my beloved editor, from whom I have learned so much; LuAnn Finnegan, for valuable insights and time; Marilyn LeVan, for important information and illustrations; Steve Phinney, for resource materials and ideas.

Also to Wanda Elliott, Karen Anderson, Michele Halseide, Lynn Dyatt, Suzanne Lumpkin, Kim Peterson, Jill Heiken, and Joni Jacques, for faithfully praying for and encouraging me. ■

The Problem with Low Self-Esteem

*How this study guide can help
you change.*

Several years ago, psychologist Dr. James
Dobson circulated questionnaires to Christian women in the United States. His goal:
to identify their major problem areas. After
compiling the results, he found low self-
esteem at the top of the list.[1]

Low self-esteem is hardly a new problem. In ancient times, the philosopher
Aristotle wrote, "Woman may be said to be an
inferior man."[2] Women have been treated as
second-class humans throughout history, and
it's devastated their self-esteem.

Although women in the United States
enjoy a more liberated status than those
in most countries, we're still evaluated by
our culture's five Bs: beauty, brains, bank
accounts, busyness, and belonging.[3]

When we succumb to this faulty assess-
ment of personal worth, we become people-

pleasers, intensely critical, performance oriented, and perfectionists. It's an inevitable formula for misery.

BETTER THAN YOU THINK

If you're hiding inferiority feelings about yourself, be encouraged. There's hope. You're really better than you think!

In God's eyes, people are the world's most important commodity, to be handled with care. To waste additional years concealing a crumbling interior flings away precious, God-given potential.

Are you weary of searching for ways to hide your secret? Are you afraid someone may reject the real you? If so, this study can begin your journey toward wholeness.

Through the article "Hidden Self-Portraits" and a self-assessment test, you'll explore the roots of low self-esteem. Then five study lessons will help you gain a clearer, more biblical view of yourself.

While it's best to read and study this entire booklet, you may want to ponder only the opening article, or you might just complete the Bible studies. In addition to personal study, consider using this guide for:

- Daily devotions.

- Sunday school classes.

- Small-group Bible studies.

- One-on-one study or discipling.

10

- Lifestyle evangelism with friends.

- Professional or coffee-cup counseling.

But remember, there are no overnight cures for low self-esteem. This study is only a start, not an instant antidote for your problems.

It takes time, God's Word, and persistent application to heal inferiority feelings. But it's worth the work. You can walk away from the pain and discover that you're better than you think! ∎

—MADALENE HARRIS

NOTES
1. James Dobson, *The Christian Woman's Search for Self-Esteem* (Nashville, TN: Thomas Nelson, 1982), page 31.
2. Bergen Evans, *Dictionary of Quotations* (New York: Delecorte Press, 1968), page 762.
3. James and Sally Conway, *Women in Mid-Life Crisis* (Wheaton, IL: Tyndale, 1983), page 207.

Hidden Self-Portraits

*Discovering why we're ashamed
of ourselves.*

Nobody could guess her secret. Gifted, well-
educated, highly productive—these words
described Anita, an executive type with a
successful counseling-and-seminar career.
Easily the envy of most women, she appeared
to lack nothing.

So when Anita confessed her lifelong
battle with low self-esteem, it shocked me.
How could anyone be so successful and
insecure at the same time? The two didn't fit
together in my mind.

"I put on a wonderful show," she
explained. "I was a hero, a high achiever,
always pushing ahead." She admitted
it wasn't easy. She covered her fear of
inadequacy with accomplishments. Her
solution was always to do more, more,
more.

"The real truth is that I was fiercely

protecting a wounded child within me by means of control," she disclosed. "If anything moved out of my control, I'd be forced to work harder. It was like trying to hold seven beach balls under water—one was always popping up."

Eventually, Anita became unapproachable. If people disagreed with her, *they* were wrong. Intimate relationships became impossible because she trusted no one.

But Anita wasn't always so untrusting. Once she was a tender girl, longing for acceptance, wanting to please, and trying to figure out why Daddy didn't seem to love her.

An unyielding controller, Anita's father had only one right way to do anything, and that was *his way*. No questions, no alternatives, no mercy. Anita doesn't remember receiving affection or approval from her father—or ever pleasing him.

But Anita does remember one event when she was seven years old. Hungry for affection and approval, she climbed into Daddy's lap to hug him. Immediately, he tore away her entwined arms and thrust her to the floor shouting, "Stop bothering me!"

From that incident, a deep woundedness crippled Anita with low self-esteem for many years. But you'd never know it. Anita kept her self-hatred tightly hidden under a mask of continual achievement.

14

Anita's story is typical of many women. Psychologists and statisticians have estimated that most women in the United States suffer from the debilitating malady of low self-esteem.

It's astonishing how few people really like themselves. Yet author and educator Leo Buscaglia points out that "self-esteem affects every aspect of our lives. It determines our happiness, our peace of mind, the relationships we have, our jobs, our job performance, how successful we become, how we influence others."[1]

These outcomes make good self-esteem vitally important. But before we can achieve it, we need to honestly admit we don't like ourselves. As long as we disguise underlying emotions, we thwart the hope for freedom from self-hatred.

A self-image dilemma is like carrying around two pictures of ourselves. Each of us presents one picture to the world and keeps one secretly hidden inside us. The hidden picture is how we view ourselves. If we ever spilled the secret-portrait for others to see, we'd be humiliated.

Still, hidden self-portraits affect our emotional and spiritual well-being. Whether we realize it or not, we usually act in harmony with these portraits. Tragically, our actions aren't based on our true potential or abilities. If we see ourselves as failures, we'll find ways to fail, no matter how much we want to succeed. We create our own self-fulfilling prophecies.

IDENTIFYING SOURCES

The reasons for low self-esteem vary as much as the individual circumstances of our lives, but usually low self-worth stems from seeds planted early. Self-hatred doesn't happen overnight; it's painfully developed through the growing-up years.

From negative messages in childhood, many of us concluded that we're not as good or capable as others. One young man expressed it by saying, "There's just something missing in me that I can't identify or ever go back and change." Most of us secretly feel the same way.

"My brother was retarded," one woman told me. "And everyone acted like something was wrong with me. Eventually I began to believe that I was mentally impaired. So I never really tried to do well in school or life. Imagine my surprise, after thirty-seven years, to discover I'm really quite brilliant and capable."

Another woman tearfully recounted her futile attempts at pleasing her mother. "Nothing I did was good enough," she said.

One day in desperation she sobbed out her love to her mother. The girl explained how much she wanted to please her mom, but she didn't know how.

"I know, child, I know," the mother replied.

16

"For a moment I thought she would at long last affirm me," said the daughter.

Instead, the mother said, "You're close, honey. Really close. Maybe someday you'll manage to make me truly happy."

Sometimes unexpected events alter our lives. My own struggle to discover self-worth began that way. I started out in a highly functional family with loving, affirming parents. But my mother died when I was eight.

After her death, I felt different from other children. I didn't have a mother to take care of my needs, to attend school functions, or to give me the nurturing I desperately longed for. I felt deprived, different, neglected, rejected. And I didn't recognize the source of my low self-worth.

The stories could continue. They'd ring with similarity about the pain and the wasted years seeking approval or acceptance somewhere—anywhere.

I couldn't identify the source of my poor self-esteem until well into adulthood. The same is true for many low self-esteem sufferers. But once these sources are identified, we can take steps toward healing and inner wholeness.

MEASURING SELF-IMAGES

Answer the question, "Who are you?" Would your answer be something like the following?

- I am John's wife.

- I am Amanda's mother.

- I am a clerk. A writer. A housewife. A lawyer. A musician.

- I am nobody special.

Self-descriptions reveal how we value ourselves. And the answers above say, "I am an extension of someone or something else. Apart from that, I can't identify myself."

Certainly there are periods in our lives where we extend into other peoples' lives. With four small children and a husband who traveled most of the time, I remember years of being "just somebody's mother." There was no time for a life of my own. I wrestled against feelings of meaninglessness and questioned my identity.

Despite my questioning, I believed there was a person of worth hidden inside me. I clung to the hope of self-discovery. Eventually, by understanding my true value, the real me emerged years later.

But it's not necessary to wait that long. We can discover and like ourselves now. We can value ourselves for who we really are—not just for what we do or who we're associated with. But it means taking a look inside ourselves.

UNCOVERING THE SHAME

"Low self-worth usually stems from feelings of shame," Anita told me. "We are living with secrets inside. We can't be open and real, so we swallow the shame and rationalize it through denial instead of dealing with the real source."

Professional counselor Robert S. McGee confirms Anita's observation. He says shame is a deep sense of inferiority that creates a permanent negative opinion about our self-worth.[2] Simply put, low self-esteem usually means we're ashamed of ourselves. And if shame is the source of low self-esteem problems, it's important to examine this emotion.

Shame is the pain we experience when something dishonorable or disgraceful happens to us. It results from our own actions or the actions of others. But at the time, we may not realize that shame has crept into mental images of ourselves.

Shame enters belief systems at a very early age, slipping into subconscious minds. Or it can overtly ravage us with words like, "Shame on you! You're a bad girl!" Heard often enough, such words can mark us for life. And if rejection by a parent hardens our hearts toward love, it's possible to feel shame at the thought of being rejected again.

Such fear turns us into wimpish people-pleasers. If we can just accomplish enough, be good enough, please enough people, we will be worthwhile. Or like Anita, we become controllers. Nobody's going to hurt us again!

The primary objective of shame is to not be exposed. Shame slips in when we feel vulnerable and threatened. Out of control. Suddenly we're exposed and in danger of losing something or someone we value highly. If we're exposed against our wills and our secret spills out, we dive deeper into low self-esteem.

To avoid exposure, shame disguises itself under a variety of cover-ups. And most people who are shame-based don't know it. Shame-based people hide behind blame, control, criticism, self-pity, depression, perfectionism, irrational rage, a performance orientation, or a preoccupation with feelings.

These masks seem like the only route to survival, and we tenaciously cling to them. So finding our root problem is like diving into the ocean for a lost coin.

HELEN'S AMAZING STORY

On and off for years, Helen had been slipping into depression. Eventually, her condition progressed so that normal functioning became impossible. Then Helen visited a counselor.

The counselor detected suppressed anger but couldn't dig out its source. So she decided to take Helen through a "life walk." With this method, Helen prayerfully reviewed her life, asking the Holy Spirit to reveal buried, hurtful memories. What turned up for Helen was amazing.

Until the seventh grade, Helen had been an excellent student. She was self-assured and popular with both teachers and peers. Because of Helen's outstanding reading skills, one day a teacher asked her to read a difficult passage to the class.

While reading, the girl sitting behind

Helen kept ridiculing her in an undertone.

"You think you're such a good reader. Well, it sounds terrible," whispered the girl. "Everybody's laughing at you."

Helen burst into tears and flew out of the room. Shame and anger swept away her confidence, and from that point, she slid downhill. Helen remembered withdrawing and never excelling at anything again.

When these deeply buried memories flooded her consciousness, the adult Helen began sobbing. Having exposed the hatred and bitterness, she finally took steps toward emotional wholeness. In a short time, her depression disappeared, and today Helen is a joyful person.

SHAME VS. GUILT

When searching for the roots of shame, they can often be mistaken for guilt. So it's important to understand the fine line of difference between shame and guilt.

Adam and Eve illustrate this difference.[3] These two deliberately chose to disobey God. Disobedience to God is sin, and as a result of their actions, Adam and Eve became guilty. So what was the first thing they did? Hide from God. Sin and guilt usually drive us into hiding.

Shame didn't enter this picture until Adam and Eve realized they were naked. This sounds strange because they'd been naked all along. But sin suddenly opened their eyes, and they felt ashamed of themselves.

So guilt results from what we *do.* (Adam and Eve ate the forbidden fruit—guilt.) Shame attacks what we *are.* (They were naked—shame.) Without question, shame and guilt often accompany one another, but a marked line of difference exists between these two feelings.

Even though shame isn't necessarily rooted in sin, it can be so mingled with guilt that we have trouble separating the two. We must pry them apart before we can deal with either. Sometimes asking the question, "Have I actually done anything wrong?" helps clarify the issue.

For example, as an innocent victim of rape, a woman may be emotionally shattered. Her shame becomes unbearable. But she is not guilty of sin. Her answer to the above question is, "No, I've done nothing wrong." With that admission, she's finally on the road to confronting reality—and her shame.

However, if we have sinned, there's a scriptural order for dealing with the guilt. These steps are:

- **Admit the sin.** The Bible states, "If we claim to be without sin, we deceive ourselves and the truth is not in us" (1 John 1:8).

- **Repent of the sin.** This means to agree with God that our action was contrary to His stated will. Scripture also asserts that God is patient with us, "not wanting anyone to perish, but everyone to come to repentance" (2 Peter 3:9).

- **Confess the sin.** First John continues: "If we confess our sins, he is faithful and just and will forgive us our sins and purify us from all unrighteousness" (verse 9).

When we sincerely take these steps, we're finished with the sin and its guilt. The slate is now clean. We may indulge in unbelief and still feel guilty, but that feeling is false guilt.

OUR ONLY HOPE

Those of us with low self-worth often have experienced one loss after another, so we're like hard-packed clay. Afraid to stay where we are, afraid to move anywhere else, we stand on the fringes of life, unable to enter the mainstream. We become emotionally frozen in time and can't heal or mature from emotional setbacks.

It's difficult for us to recover from accidents or illnesses, betrayal by a trusted friend, the loss of a job or a deserved promotion, conflicts in relationships, or other disappointments. Trauma and rejection stay locked in our minds, along with a rotten opinion of ourselves.

Reasons may vary, but the current secular emphasis on self-worth obscures the true source of our wholeness. That is, *healthy self-esteem originates with God.*

The fall of humanity and the introduction of sin robbed us of emotional stability. Because of sin, we are depraved people, with no hope of emotional or spiritual wholeness. So the healing we seek begins with the divine miracle of Christ's sacrifice on the cross and the forgiveness of our sins.

It is only through God's grace that any of us dares to believe we are acceptable. It's the righteousness of Jesus Christ that affords our claim to wholeness. Apart from Him, we have no hope of anything except condemnation.

Forgiveness through Jesus Christ is our gateway to freedom. His righteousness, living within us, is our promise for a healthy self-image.

With God's help, we can be free from the prison of low self-esteem. But it's up to us to plant our feet firmly on the path toward healing. Once we're on that journey, all of God's supernatural power is available to heal, mature, and release us.

It's not an overnight trip; it's more of an ongoing quest. And the first step is honestly acknowledging the pain that keeps our low self-worth virus alive.

That's where Anita started. Her life story read like a tragedy of drowning hopes and unfulfilled desires. Then one day she peeked out of her darkness, gathered courage enough to reach out for help, and eventually walked into freedom. Today Anita is not only healed, but God uses her to help other hurting people.

God plays no favorites with people.[5]
Anita would say that if He healed her low
self-esteem, He can change anyone.
And that anyone can be you. ∎

NOTES
1. Leo Buscaglia, "There's No One in the World Like You,"
   Woman's Day, March 29, 1988, page 28.
2. Robert S. McGee, *The Search for Significance* (Houston,
   TX: Rapha Publishing, 1987).
3. Genesis 3:6-7.
4. Romans 2:11.

The Big Coverup

*Facing behaviors that hide
inferiority feelings.*

If you don't like yourself, there's a reason.
You're probably still harboring negative messages from childhood. And like Anita, you
may have pushed inferiority feelings deep
inside yourself.

But like it or not, your actions are probably giving away your true feelings.

1. Read the list below, and check each
   statement that applies to you.

   ___ I set high standards for myself. (A)
   ___ The fear of failure keeps me from
       things I'd like to do. (A)
   ___ I'm depressed when I fail to meet
       other people's expectations. (A)
   ___ I work harder than anyone I know,
       but I still don't feel good about
       myself. (A)

___ I fear what other people think of me. (B)

___ If significant people in my life disapprove of me, I don't feel worthwhile. (B)

___ I don't like some of the things I do to please others, but I'm afraid of rejection and don't stop. (B)

___ If somebody corrects me, I feel defensive and it destroys our relationship. (B)

___ I'm not content unless everything is in order. (C)

___ No matter how well I do something, I'm never pleased. (C)

___ If my work and surroundings aren't perfect, it upsets me. (C)

___ I drive myself and others to perform perfectly. (C)

___ Emotional people appear weak to me. (D)

___ I would like to trust God more, but I can't. (D)

___ I'm uncomfortable with close relationships. (D)

___ I get angry when people don't conform to my way of doing things. (D)

Now add the number of checks you marked for statements with these letters behind them:

___A ___B ___C ___D

All of the behaviors in this list can be based on low self-esteem. If you checked more than one statement for any letter, you may be covering up poor self-esteem with shame-based behavior patterns.

LOW SELF-ESTEEM PATTERNS

2. Read the following descriptions, paying particular attention to the letters you checked most often. Then check the patterns that best describe you.

___ **A. Performance orientation: basing self-worth on accomplishments.** This behavior is born from the unrealistic demands, expectations, and intimidations of others. A fear of failure creates a "measure-up complex" and deceptively promises that good performance will gain acceptance and love. These people work hard to meet self-imposed standards in order to feel good about themselves.

___ **B. Approval addiction: basing self-worth on the opinions of others.** These people become whatever it takes to receive approval. A fear of rejection drives them to comply with impossible-to-please persons and difficult circumstances. They require constant affirmation and usually respond defensively to reproofs.

___ **C. Perfectionism: discontent-
ment with anything that is
not nearly perfect.** Because
perfectionists do things well, they
are often admired and sought
after. But perfectionists harbor the
compulsive need to prove themselves, and they feel they're never
doing well enough. Anxiety and
self-depreciation dominate their
continual striving for the impossible. A fear of condemnation moti-
vates them.

___ **D. Control: the inability to
cope and the drive to dominate if things or people do
not cooperate.** Risk of failure
or vulnerability can trigger an
intense fear of not being in control. Often these people are out of
touch with their emotions. They
have difficulty trusting God or
people. Controllers adhere to rigid
rules and overly emphasize do's
and don'ts.

NEGATIVE ACTIONS

Within these four shame-based patterns,
negative actions emerge that vary according to individual dispositions and life
circumstances.

3. Check the actions that may apply
   to you.

___ **Blame:** making someone else the scapegoat for personal failures.

___ **Compulsiveness:** an obsessive need to achieve, conform, or perform contrary to will or ability.

___ **Denial:** an inability or unwillingness to face the truth.

___ **Dependence:** transferring decisions and responsibilities to another person to avoid failure.

___ **Overachievement/underachievement:** the need to perform for acceptance.

___ **Rage:** unreasonable anger over a loss of control.

___ **Rationalization:** crediting actions to the wrong causes.

___ **Secretiveness:** concealing memories or inadequacies.

___ **Self-consciousness:** excessive awareness that others may be observing personal actions.

___ **Withdrawal:** removing from active participation to hide feelings of inadequacy.

ASKING FOR HELP

4. Did you find yourself in any of the low self-esteem patterns or actions? Describe how you feel about your discovery.

Even if you exhibit all of these behaviors, take heart. This self-discovery can initiate your walk toward emotional wholeness. It's a journey you don't have to take alone. God and friends, family, or counselors can guide you each step of the way.

5. List people who could help you face your low self-esteem behaviors. How could each one help you?

6. Write a prayer, asking God to help you overcome poor self-esteem. Then plan how to ask the people you listed for their help.

7. Copy the prayer on a 3″ x 5″ card and post it somewhere you can say it every day while facing your self-esteem problem. ■

God Doesn't Carry a Big Stick

*Learn to accept who you are in
His eyes.*

S T E P   O N E

To accept myself, I will believe God
loves me and created me the way I am.

A friend once told me, "Even though I've gone
to church all my life, I never once heard that
God was *for* me. I'd always thought He was a
harsh judge, eagerly waiting to pounce on me
for any misstep."

How sad, but tragically true, that many
of us grew up feeling like God carries a big
stick. And we still live as if we're afraid He's
going to whack us.

The truth is that God loves us uncon-
ditionally. In Jeremiah 31:3-4, He said, "I
have loved you with an everlasting love;
I have drawn you with loving-kindness.
I will build you up again and you will be
rebuilt."

If you've been emotionally wounded, it's
probably difficult to believe that God loves
you. And good self-esteem begins with understanding His opinion of you.

1. Read the statements below. Circle the ones that describe how you feel about yourself when the low self-esteem virus hits.

   Now read Psalm 139. Based on this chapter, check whether the following statements are true or false. Write down the verse number that supports your answer.

   T F
   ❏ ❏ I am a biological accident.

   ❏ ❏ God is not concerned with my problems.

   ❏ ❏ God doesn't understand my inner pain.

   ❏ ❏ I can hide my feelings from God.

   ❏ ❏ God doesn't hear me when I pray.

   ❏ ❏ I can never be good enough for God.

   ❏ ❏ If I could change myself, God would be more pleased with me.

2. Psalm 139:14 declares that you are "fear-fully and wonderfully made." Describe your feelings about this claim.

GOD CLAIMS YOU

3. According to the following verses, write God's description of who you are.

John 15:13-14

Romans 8:17

1 Peter 2:9

4. Combining what you've read in Psalm 139 and these verses, write a paragraph about your spiritual identity.

GOD ACCEPTS YOU

As a child, you may have learned that if you didn't perform, you weren't accepted. So it wasn't difficult to transfer that concept into adulthood. Only now you're trying to please God instead of parents. That's why it's important to understand His acceptance of you.

5. According to these verses, how has God shown that He accepts you?

Romans 5:8-10

Titus 3:6-7

GOD GIVES TO YOU

6. From the following verses, list the things God says you possess as His child.

Romans 5:1

Therefore, since we have been justified through faith, we have peace with God through our Lord Jesus Christ

Romans 8:1

Therefore, there is now no condemnation for those who are in Christ Jesus, because thru Jesus the law of the spirit of life, set me free from the law of sin & death.

Ephesians 1:3

Praise be to the God and Father of our Lord Jesus Christ, who has blessed us in the heavenly realms with every spiritual blessing in Christ.

Colossians 2:9-10

For in Christ all the fullness of the Deity lives in bodily form, and you have been given fullness in Christ, who is the head 37 over every power and authority.

7. What can you do to help yourself really believe God's high opinion of you?

8. Write a concluding prayer, asking God to help you see yourself as He created you—in His image.

GOD LOVES YOU

This week, use a Bible concordance to find more verses about God's love for you. Memorize the one that most comforts you. ■

If God is for us, who can be against us?
(Romans 8:31)

Don't Hold Yourself Hostage!

*Forgive the people who hurt
your self-image.*

S T E P   T W O
I will prepare myself to forgive the people who caused my shame.

In America's recent memory, fifty-two citizens were held hostage in Iran for more than a year. President Jimmy Carter flew to Wiesbaden, Germany, to greet the returning hostages when they were released.

At that time, Carter told the press that "our Americans were mistreated much worse than was previously believed."[1] The hostages confirmed they were subjected to mock firing squads, games of Russian roulette, and forms of mental and physical torture.

These citizens of a free country were powerless to resist whatever indignities the enemy perpetrated. Until their release, they remained at the mercy of the Iranian government.

As a citizen of God's Kingdom, you've been given freedom from sin (John 8:32, Romans 6:18). But you can be an emotional captive of your past by not forgiving people or circumstances that hurt you. This allows Satan, your spiritual enemy, to torment you with anger, hatred, revenge, and bitterness.

But unlike the American hostages, you can choose whether you'll be held captive. The path to freedom is forgiveness. Joseph's captivity in Egypt illustrates this point.

THE BROTHERS' OFFENSE

1. Read Genesis 37:1-4. In your opinion, whose attitudes were wrong? Did Joseph do anything wrong?

   Joseph's brothers attitudes were wrong. Joseph did not do anything wrong

2. Now read Genesis 37:17-28.

   a. How do you feel about the brothers' actions?

   Reuben tried to rescue Joseph but his brothers hated him so much. They were eating when the Ishmaelites came by, their hate was so great it didn't even affect their appetite.

40

b. Why would they resort to such
   measures?

because of hate toward Joseph

JOSEPH'S ATTITUDE

3. Describe how Joseph must have felt during this ordeal.

alone, betrayed

4. According to Genesis 39:4-23, how did
   Joseph respond to his afflictions during
   confinement?

Pretty good, the Lord was with him and showed him kindness + granted him favor in the eyes of the prison warden

5. What was God's response to Joseph?

God showed Joseph kindness and the Lord was w/ him in prison.

6. Now turn to Genesis 45:4-15. After a lifetime of alienation from family and country, what was Joseph's attitude toward his brothers?

    He welcomed them.
    Weep, embraced them
    and blessed them all.

7. Read Genesis 50:19-21 and consider Joseph's words.

    a. Why was Joseph able to fully forgive his brothers?

    because it accomplished
    what God intended it to
    accomplish.

    b. How did his forgiveness relate to God's plans?

    Joseph knew God
    intended to accomplish
    saving many lives.

8. What are your honest feelings about
   Joseph's act of forgiveness?

   awesome —

YOUR RESPONSE

9. Write a paragraph that compares your
   past painful circumstances to Joseph's
   story. (How have you been treated un-
   fairly? How did you feel?)

10. Read Matthew 6:14-15, Ephesians 4:32,
    and Colossians 3:13. How could God's
    forgiveness be wrapped in your decision
    to forgive people who have hurt you?

   *FOR IF you forgive men when they
   in against you, your heavenly Father will
   so forgive you. But if you do not forgive men
   heir sins, Your Father will not forgive
   ur sins.*

   *Be kind and compassionate to one
   other, forgiving each other, just as in
   rist God forgave you.*

11. How could forgiving these people affect your low self-esteem?

12. Are you *willing* to forgive these people so you can be healed? If so, write a statement of commitment to forgive them.

GETTING READY

Now that you understand the importance of forgiveness, spend this week praying about and answering these questions.

- Am I aware of the people I need to forgive? Who are they?

- Am I willing to let God show me the people I'm not aware of?

- What could happen if I choose not to forgive them?

- What could happen if I do forgive them? ∎

NOTE
1. Clifton Daniel, ed., *Chronicles of America* (Mount Kiseo, NY: Chronicle Publications, n.d.), page 870.

"Father, forgive them, for they do not know what they are doing."
(Luke 23:34)

Colossians 3:13

Bear with each other and forgive whatever grievances you may have against one another. Forgive as the Lord forgave you.

Searching for Roots

*Walk through the shame
toward freedom.*

S   T   E   P   T   H   R   E   E
I will search for the roots of my shame and forgive the people who caused it.

Remember Helen, whose repressed shame caused her depression? (See page 20.) She discovered that the only way to overcome shame is to face it and to feel the pain.

A psalmist said, "It was good for me to be afflicted so that I might learn your decrees" (Psalm 119:71). Learning to obey God—and finding the wholeness you crave—often results from inward pain.

Shameful secrets feel safer when they're hidden, and you can keep them submerged in you forever. But you'll never experience freedom from poor self-esteem. The risk of exposure is the initial step for tracing shame in your life.

Like Helen, a "life walk" may help you find the roots of your shame. The following guidelines will help you face the shame so you can be healed from it.

A life walk begins with making an emotional inventory of your memories. You may complete this inventory by yourself or with a trusted friend.

1. Prayerfully review Daniel 2:22 and Luke 8:17. How are secrets of our hearts revealed?

For there is nothing hidden that will not be disclosed, and nothing concealed that will not be known or brought out into the open.

2. What methods could God use to reveal hidden things of your past?

3. How do you feel about what God might reveal to you?

4. Begin by asking God to help you face whatever He shows you. Then prayerfully review your life, asking the Holy Spirit to reveal painful incidents that

48

hurt your self-esteem.

As memories come to mind, make a list of them. Include the events and people responsible for them. It may take several days and the reliving of painful episodes, but this is necessary for healing. (You may need another sheet of paper for this exercise.)

EVENTS	PEOPLE

5. Once your list is complete, you need to review the difference between guilt and shame. (See page 21.) From your understanding of this difference, fill in the following chart.

GUILT	SHAME
Definition	
When It Occurs	
Solution	

6. Review your inventory list in question 4, and indicate whether each incident involved true guilt (mark with a "G") or shame (mark with an "S"). Remember

to ask yourself, "Did I do anything wrong?"

7. On the entries marked "G," sincerely confess the sin to God. To help you during confession, write 1 John 1:9 below.

If we confess our sins, he is faithful + just and will forgive us our sins and purify us from all unrighteousness.

8. a. Now read Hebrews 12:2. What does this verse say about shame?

   b. How did Christ's shame affect the shame you feel today?

FORGIVING THE SHAME

For each remaining item marked "S," ask the Lord to heal the hurt and shame you experienced. One by one, apply what you learned

in lesson 2 and forgive the people who caused
your shame and pain.

Even though you were guilty of no sin,
your reaction to shame can be sinful (i.e.,
anger, hatred, bitterness). If you've had sinful reactions to shameful experiences, confess
those to God, too.

ACCEPTING UNCHANGEABLES

Not all shame is caused by people. Sometimes we're ashamed of circumstances
beyond our control. For example, age, gender,
parents, birth order, siblings, mental abilities, and physical features. These can lower
our self-esteem.

9. List the unchangeable things about your
   life that you've never accepted. Explain
   why they've caused you shame.

UNCHANGEABLES	SHAME

Sincerely surrender to God any resentment toward these unchangeable aspects of your life. Name each feature and confess your sinful response to it. Forgive those you may have blamed for the circumstances: God, parents, yourself.

FORGETTING THE PAST

10. Read Philippians 3:13-14.

    a. Why is it important to forget the past?

Paul said forgetting what is behind and straining toward what is ahead.

    b. How does this apply to you?

11. Read Philippians 3:13-14 again. If you continue carrying painful memories, what might happen?

You won't press on toward the goal to win the prize for which God has called me heavenward in Christ Jesus.

12. Now that you have confessed sin and asked for healing, how can you put the past behind you? List at least three things you can begin doing this week.

FINDING THE STRENGTH

This week, memorize Philippians 4:13: "I can do everything through him who gives me strength."

If you begin to doubt whether the past is now behind you—that God is healing you from shame—quote this promise and believe that God is transforming you. ■

Because the Sovereign LORD helps me,
I will not be disgraced.
Therefore have I set my face like flint,
and I know I will not be put to shame.
(Isaiah 50:7)

Oh, Those Little Lies!

*Stop saying negative things
about yourself.*

S   T   E   P   F   O   U   R
I will combat negative self-talk from Satan, myself, and others.

The word *sabotage* originated through dramatic events in France during the 1880s. No labor unions existed, so French workers would complain against unjust taskmasters with the *sabots* (wooden shoes) on their feet.

When employers wouldn't listen or negotiate, irate workers ripped off their *sabots,* angrily flung them into machinery, and stalked out of the workplace. These workers became known as *sabot-eurs.*

Nobody will be throwing wooden shoes at you, but saboteurs of your soul will threaten to thwart your progress toward wholeness. Often the saboteur will be Satan. Sometimes they will be people. Other times, you will be your own worst enemy. At all times, you must be on your guard against these destroyers.

Because you have been hearing and

reinforcing low self-esteem messages for so
long, it won't be easy to eliminate them. But
to walk free from a poor self-image, these
saboteurs must be silenced.

RECOGNIZE THE LIE

1. Satan began his deceptive tactics with
   Eve in the Garden of Eden. You probably
   know the story, but review how Satan
   deceived her. What did he say to Eve in
   Genesis 3:1-5?

*God knows that when you eat of
it your eyes will be opened, &
you will be like God, knowing
good & evil.*

2. Now read Genesis 3:6.

   a. What three observations persuaded
      Eve to disobey God?

*pleasing to the eye,
tree was good for food
desirable for gaining wisdom*

   b. What personal observations would
      keep you from following God toward
      emotional wholeness?

3. Read how Jesus described Satan in
   John 8:44. Based on Eve's experience
   and Jesus' words, write scenarios for
   how Satan might deceive you about past
   shame and/or people you've forgiven.

Satan has no truth in
him. He speaks his native
language which is lies &
the father of lies.

4. From 1 Peter 5:8-9, what is your responsibility toward combatting Satan's lies?

Be self-controlled and alert.
Your enemy the devil prowls around like
a roaring lion looking for someone to devour.
Resist him, Stand firm in the faith.

A prayer such as this one can help you
begin combatting Satan's deception:

*Father God, please open my eyes to
Satan's deceptive schemes. Help me to
detect his lies as soon as I start thinking
them. I determine, with Your help, to stop
believing his counterfeit and place my
confidence in Your truth as revealed in
Your Word.*

To "devour" you, Satan often attacks your thoughts. He loves to feed you false messages about your self-worth: "I'm no good"; "I can't do anything right"; "I'm not as smart as others"; "I'm a failure"; "I'll never amount to anything"; "Even God is disappointed with me." Satan plays on messages you've told yourself in the past.

To resist negative ideas, you can counteract them by thought interruption. Simple commands will do the trick, such as saying aloud, "Satan is a liar. I refuse to listen."

Sometimes you're the originator of negative putdowns. The important thing is to stop the lies before they dominate your mind. Deal firmly with yourself and the enemy.

RENEW YOUR MIND

5. As you learn to detect and interrupt false inner dialogue, you need to replace negative thoughts with God's truth. According to Romans 12:2, why is it important to "renew your mind"?

So I can test and approve what God's will is — his good, pleasing + perfect will.

6. The following verses give insight on how to renew your mind and life. How can these verses apply to you?

Psalm 1:1-3 meditate on God's word day + night. A righteous man does not believe like, behave like, or belong to the realm of wicked men.

Psalm 119:37

turn my eyes away from worthless things, perserve my life according to your word.

Psalm 119:45

I will walk about in freedom for I have sought out your percepts

Psalm 119:107

I have suffered much; perserve my life, O Lord, according to your word.

7. Renewing your mind is a spiritual battle. According to 2 Corinthians 10:4-5 and Ephesians 6:10-18, describe the weapons you'll need to use and the strongholds they will destroy.

the weapons we fight with are not weapons of the world, they have divine power to demolish strongholds
We take captive every thought to make it obedient to Christ.

The Full Armor of God, so you can stand against the devil's schemes.
Belt of truth – breastplate of R – gospel of peace

8. Since Satan is a liar and God is truth (John 8:44, 14:6), you need to begin listening to God's words about you. Review lesson 1 to remember His opinion of you. What else does the Lord say about who you are—now and in the future?

2 Corinthians 5:17

Ephesians 2:10

Philippians 3:12

9. List the lies that you, Satan, or others may tell you about yourself. Then from what you've learned in this study, counteract each one with God's truth.

LIES	GOD'S TRUTH

RISK ACCOUNTABILITY

You don't have to battle Satan alone. In
addition to God's help, you can draw strength
and encouragement from another believer
recovering from low self-esteem. Or you
might find a support group of three or more.

10. Read and consider Galatians 6:2.

   a. What's one reason you should get
      together with other believers?

   *to carry each others
   burdens, and in this way
   you will fullfill the law
   of Christ.*

b. Why would this be important?

If your low-self-esteem problem has been hidden, accountability may sound frightening. But it will be important for changing your life's direction.

11. In the following verses, record what happens when you "go it alone" versus seeking counsel.

WITHOUT COUNSEL	WITH COUNSEL
Proverbs 11:14	For lack of guidance a nation falls, but many advisors make victory sure.
Proverbs 12:15	The plans of the righteous are just, but the advice of the wicked is deceitful.

WITHOUT COUNSEL	WITH COUNSEL
Proverbs 13:10	*Pride only breeds quarrels, but wisdom is found in those who take advice.*
Proverbs 15:22	*Plans fail for lack of counsel but w/ many advisers they succeed.*

12. Describe what type of person(s) you'll need to help you recover from low self-esteem.

LOOKING FOR COUNSEL

Before jumping into an accountability relationship, follow these guidelines.

- **Pray for God's wisdom.** Wait for His direction.

- **Make your partner a woman.** This will increase mutual understanding and avoid inappropriate attraction to the opposite sex.

- **Meet regularly.** Share victories as well as defeats. Pray for each other daily and while meeting together.

This week, begin praying for an accountability partner, using the description you wrote in question 12. ■

With you is the fountain of life;
in your light we see light.
(Psalm 36:9)

One Day at a Time

Begin recovery with the improved you.

S T E P   F I V E

With God's help, I will begin again
with a new image of myself.

After murdering a man in Egypt, Moses fled
to a desert and hid himself for forty years. He
probably planned to spend the rest of his life
tending sheep there. After all, he was eighty.

But God had different ideas. He chose
Moses to accomplish an amazing exploit:
rescuing several million people from the iron
grip of Egypt's king.

For years, Moses had been haunted
by the memory of his shameful act. His
self-esteem must have been lower than a
desert snake, slithering across the ground.
But our God is the Lord of new begin-
nings. He wouldn't let Moses wiggle out of a
divinely appointed task. (Read and consider
Exodus 3.)

God can transform miserable dropouts
into examples of His grace. That's what He's
ready to do for you.

SEE YOUR POTENTIAL

If the God who created you says something about your identity, isn't He to be trusted beyond how you feel about yourself? Or what anyone else says about you? Only in the Bible can you glimpse your full potential.

1. What does God say about your potential to change?

   Matthew 19:26 with man this is impossible, but with God all things are possible.

   Romans 8:37

   No, in all these things we are more than conquerors through him who loved us.

   Philippians 4:13

   I can do everything through him who gives me strength.

   Philippians 4:19

   And my God will meet all your needs according to his glorious riches in Christ Jesus.

2. Write a brief, personal response to these verses. State how your life would change, if you'd really believe these verses.

AFFIRM GOD'S PROMISES

One reading is not enough. Turning God's promises into daily affirmations keeps them fresh in your mind.

3. Choose two of the promises in question 1 and write them below. After each verse, describe how it offers you hope for walking away from low self-esteem.

4. God offers His help and restoration, but you have a part to play in the process. According to these verses, what will God do? What should be your response?

GOD'S PROMISE	MY RESPONSE
Joshua 1:8-9	Have I not command you? Be strong and courageous. Do not be afraid, don't be discourage, for the Lord your God is with you
Isaiah 42:6,9	The Lord called us to righteousness. I will take hold of your hand.
Isaiah 43:18-19	Forget the former things do not dwell on the past. See I am doing a new thing etc.....
Joel 2:25-26	I will repay you for the years the locusts have eaten — You will have plenty to eat, until you are full, and you will praise the name of the Lord your God who has worked wonders for you never again will my people be shamed

5. a. What daily comfort can you draw from these verses?

   b. What daily actions could make them come true in your life?

ONE DAY AT A TIME

My friend Anita, who describes herself as a "recovering Nero," told me she can live only one day at a time. No more.

She says, "I can only say that today I am not a controller. I've made the choice for today to let God be in control. Beyond that, I can't boast."

6. The Bible confirms Anita's statement. In Matthew 6:34, what does Jesus say about this one-day-at-a-time principle?

Do not worry about tomarrow
for tomarrow will worry about
itself. Each day has enough
trouble of 69 its own.
Worry is an indictment against the Fatherhood

7. Now turn to James 4:13-15. What additional information about daily living do you find in this passage?

8. How can you apply these principles to your battle with low self-esteem? State practical examples.

Some days, Anita finds it takes a recommitment every hour. Other days, once is enough. She says it's like being a recovering alcoholic. A lifetime of conquering her shame-based behavior is too much to contemplate. But changing one day at a time seems manageable.

9. Review the shame-based patterns you explored in the section, "The Big Coverup," on pages 29-30. Using the format on page 72 at the end of this lesson, (1) write the name of the behavior, (2) one thing you can do to combat it today, and (3) a promise from God that

He will help you. You can make multiple photocopies of this chart and use them as you continue your recovery from low self-esteem.

10. Are you ready to commit yourself to whatever it takes to walk in freedom? If you can honestly and prayerfully take this step, sign your name to the following statement. Read it often as a reminder.

I want to recover from low self-esteem. With God to help me, I will take the necessary steps to overcome my problem—no matter how long it takes. I am beginning today.

Signed:

KEEPING ON

Don't stop your journey after these lessons. With your accountability partner(s), practice the principles in this booklet. ■

"I will repay you for the years the locusts have eaten."
(Joel 2:25)

ONE DAY AT A TIME

Date:

Shame-based behavior:

What I can do to combat it today:

What I can't do anything about, but can relinquish to God:

A promise from God's Word to help me:

Getting Better Together

Questions for small groups.

LESSON 1

1. Growing up, what was your image of God? How did you develop that image?
2. Why do people often view God as a harsh judge?
3. How does our view of God affect our self-esteem?
4. What is a biblical view of God?
5. What is a biblical view of ourselves?
6. If we're "saved by grace" (Ephesians 2:8-9), why do we still link our performance to acceptance by God and others? How do we do this?
7. Is it sinful to have a poor self-image? In addition to the shame-based patterns, what other negative behaviors can a poor self-image produce?
8. Can we risk too much emphasis on good self-esteem? Explain.

9. What blocks us from accepting God's opinion of us?
10. Can a poor self-image be an excuse for not taking responsibility for ourselves? Explain.

LESSON 2

1. Can we allow ourselves to become victims of other people's actions? Explain.
2. What is the biblical response when others hurt or belittle us?
3. How does a biblical response relate to victimization?
4. What are the most difficult actions to forgive? Are there examples of this type of forgiveness in the Bible?
5. Can other qualities be mistaken for forgiveness? (For example: avoidance, denial, passiveness.) Explain.
6. Have we really forgiven people if our bitterness toward them returns after a prayer of confession? Explain.
7. Does the world respect forgiving people? Do Christians? Explain.
8. What do we have to relinquish to be forgiving people?
9. Practically speaking, how can we forgive someone who keeps hurting us?
10. What are the physical, emotional, and spiritual results of unforgiveness?

LESSON 3

1. What does shame feel like?
2. What are the risks of exposing shame?

3. How are shame-based patterns encouraged in our society?
4. If we don't expose our shame, will it eventually be revealed? Explain.
5. Why and how do we hide painful experiences in our memories?
6. Do you believe God surfaces these memories? Explain.
7. Can we feel shame if no shameful actions have hurt us? Explain.
8. What are the benefits and dangers of a "life walk"?
9. Why do we focus on and feel shame over the unchangeable aspects of our lives?
10. How can denial be mistaken for "forgetting the past"?

LESSON 4

1. Why do we believe Satan's and other people's lies about us? How can we detect them?
2. Why do we engage in negative self-talk?
3. Can pride and negative self-talk be related to each other? Explain.
4. Can pride and negative self-talk be mistaken for humility? Or vice versa? Explain.
5. Which is easier: to engage in spiritual warfare, or to suffer with low self-esteem? Explain.
6. What are practical ways we can engage in spiritual warfare against low self-esteem?
7. When are we most susceptible to lies

about ourselves? What can we do about this?

8. Why does God allow spiritual warfare against us?

9. What are the benefits and pitfalls of accountability?

10. How can control be mistaken for account-ability?

LESSON 5

1. Why do we feel there's no hope for us after failure?

2. How can failure be used to develop better self-esteem?

3. In Christ, do all people have the same potential? Explain.

4. If God can supernaturally change us, why do we need to participate in our healing?

5. How can God's promises become real and practical for us?

6. Does the one-day-at-a-time philosophy fit our culture? Explain.

7. Why is it difficult to live one day at a time?

8. When are we most susceptible to shame-based behaviors?

9. Will we ever be free from our shame-based behaviors and low self-esteem? Explain.

10. How can we continue to practice the principles from this study? ■

BIBLIOGRAPHY

Resources
for Recovery

Books for further help and study.

Blitchington, Peter W. *The Christian Woman's Search for Significance.* Nashville, TN: Thomas Nelson, 1982.

Bradshaw, John. *Healing the Shame That Binds.* Deerfield Beach, FL: Health Communications, 1988.

Heitritter, Lynn, and Jeanette Vought. *Helping Victims of Sexual Abuse.* Minneapolis, MN: Bethany, 1989.

Kurtz, Ernest, Ph.D. *Shame and Guilt.* Center City, MN: Hazelden Foundation, 1981.

McGee, Robert S. *The Search for Significance.* Houston, TX: Rapha Publishing, 1987.

Seamands, Grace. *Healing Grace*. Wheaton, IL: Victor, 1988.

Wright, Norman H. *Making Peace With Your Past*. Old Tappan, NJ: Revell, 1985. ∎

A U T H O R

Madalene Harris has co-written and published three books: *The Moon Is Not Enough*; *Lonely, But Never Alone*; and *Dreaming and Achieving the Impossible*. In addition, she has published the book *Climbing Higher* and numerous articles in a variety of magazines.

Madalene is the founder and president of Colorado Christian Communicators in Colorado Springs, Colorado, and directs the Colorado Christian Writers Conference. She also speaks at women's retreats and conferences.

The mother of four grown children, Madalene and her husband, Harlan, live in Manitou Springs, Colorado. ■

OTHER TITLES IN THIS SERIES

Additional *CRISISPOINTS* Bible studies
include:

> *Getting a Grip on Guilt* by Judith
> Couchman. Learn to live a life free
> from guilt.
>
> *Nobody's Perfect, So Why Do I Try to Be?*
> by Nancy Groom. Get over the need to do
> everything right.
>
> *So What If You've Failed?* by Penelope J.
> Stokes. Use your mistakes to become a
> more loving, godly woman.
>
> *When You Can't Get Along* by Gloria
> Chisholm. How to resolve conflict
> according to the Bible.
>
> *When Your Marriage Disappoints You*
> by Janet Chester Bly. Hope and help for
> improving your marriage.

These studies can be purchased at a
Christian bookstore. Or order a catalog from
NavPress, Customer Services, P. O. Box
6000, Colorado Springs, CO 80934. Or call
1-800-366-7788 for information. ■